Daughter, your love is a blessing every day. Thank you for allowing me into your inner world to share your hopes and dreams... for teaching me as much as I have taught you... and for bringing so much love into my life.

Titles by Marci
Published by
Blue Mountain Arts®

Angels Are Everywhere!
Angels Bring a Message
of Hope Whenever It Is Needed

Friends Are Forever
A Gift of Inspirational Thoughts
to Thank You for Being
My Friend

10 Simple Things to Remember
An Inspiring Guide to
Understanding Life

To My Daughter
Love and Encouragement
to Carry with You on Your
Journey Through Life

To My Granddaughter
A Gift of Love and Wisdom
to Always Carry
in Your Heart

To My Mother
I Will Always Carry
Your Love in My Heart

To My Sister
A Gift of Love and Inspiration
to Thank You
for Being My Sister

To My Son
Love and Encouragement
to Carry with You on Your
Journey Through Life

You Are My "Once in a Lifetime"
I Will Always Love You

To My Daughter

Love and Encouragement to carry with you on your Journey Through Life

Marci

Blue Mountain Press™
Boulder, Colorado

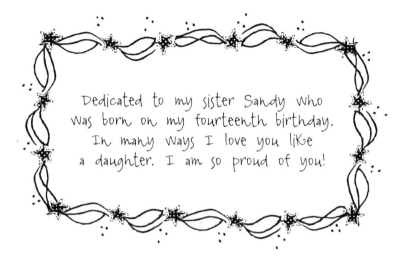

Dedicated to my sister Sandy who was born on my fourteenth birthday. In many ways I love you like a daughter. I am so proud of you!

Library of Congress Control Number: 2011905793
ISBN: 978-1-68088-140-0 (previously ISBN: 978-1-59842-620-5)

Children of the Inner Light is a registered trademark. Used under license.
Certain trademarks are used under license.

Printed in China.
Fourth printing of this edition: 2018

♻ This book is printed on recycled paper.

This book is printed on paper that has been specially produced to be acid free (neutral pH) and contains no groundwood or unbleached pulp. It conforms with the requirements of the American National Standards Institute, Inc., so as to ensure that this book will last and be enjoyed by future generations.

Blue Mountain Arts, Inc.
P.O. Box 4549, Boulder, Colorado 80306

Contents

A Daughter's Love

Is a Lifelong Blessing

Daughter, your birth was a joy and a blessing! Having you in my life has provided me with my greatest opportunity for growth, and for that I am grateful. Watching you grow and develop has provided me with some of my greatest joys. Watching you learn from your journey has taught me how to let go. Your talents and potential are extraordinary, and I give thanks for the gift of being your parent.

I Always
Wanted a
Daughter

like you

I always wanted a daughter...
someone to share wisdom and hope
with... someone to love and encourage
through life's challenges... someone to
be proud of, as I watched dreams be
fulfilled and wishes come true. What
a wonderful feeling to know I have
what I always wanted... in you!

From the first moment I laid eyes on you, we made a connection. You have brought a love and joy to my life that only a parent could know. I watched you grow and have come to understand that our lives have been brought together for a reason. I have learned as much from you as you have from me. Thank you for your love and for sharing all that is uniquely you. The bond we have found is everlasting.

The Story of Your Birth Is a Story of Joy

So often, I look back and think about the day you were born. There was so much joy at the news that you were on the way and so much anticipation about what the future would bring. Hopes and dreams were formed... love was strong... our hearts were open and ready.

♥

♥

I had a sense before you were born that you already knew who you were... I was so right! You came into the world with a strong spirit ready to learn... a kind heart ready to give... and a gentle soul ready to love. No child has ever been loved or wanted more.

Dear Daughter...

You changed My Life for the Better

Being a parent has changed my life in ways that are hard to describe. The love I feel for you is stronger than I ever dreamed possible, and the sense of responsibility is larger than I ever imagined. When I look at you, I see the future about to unfold. I want so much for you to find your place in the world... to understand the meaning of love... to know the satisfaction found in relationships. I'm grateful to have been touched by God's hand when He gave you to me as my daughter.

I'm So Glad
You Are My Child

When I became a parent, I expected to love you... I wasn't prepared to experience love in a whole new way that I never knew existed!

When I became a parent, I expected to care about your well-being... I found that caring for you became the most important thing in my life.

When I became a parent, I thought I knew all about life... but you taught me about a whole new world — a world where hopes and dreams were new... where the sacrifices of parenthood called me to be more than I ever thought I could be... and where I experienced a connection that allowed me to understand the purpose of life. I am so glad you are my child.

Daughter,
You Have Given Me

So Many Beautiful
Memories

We receive many gifts throughout our lives, and in time, we realize that the most precious gifts are the tiny special moments that live in our hearts and make us who we are. You have given me so many of those memories to save... I was there to hear your first heartbeat... I was there to watch you take your first steps... I saw you develop friendships, learn from mistakes, and grab on to independence... I am so grateful to be watching and sharing your journey.

A
Daughter's Love

Is Forever

A daughter is a gift of hopes and dreams wrapped up in a beautiful life.

A daughter is an opportunity to reflect upon the past and a chance to see possibilities fulfilled.

A daughter carries hopes from the past and dreams of the future in her heart...

A daughter's path is hers to walk;
a daughter's dreams are hers to create;
a daughter's happiness is hers to define.

A daughter is understanding, kind,
compassionate, caring, and giving.

A daughter reminds you of how much
you are loved.

A daughter is a precious gift that is unwrapped a little bit each year.

A daughter shares the journey of life, celebrating love and joy and tears and hopes as only a woman can.

A daughter's love remains forever in your heart.

Please Remember This, Daughter...

Home

The Road of Life Has Many Turns

Sometimes the road of life will take you to a place you had planned... Sometimes it will show you a surprise around the bend you could never have anticipated. You must make decisions based on the information you have... accept the ups and downs as they come... and live "one day at a time." Often you will find it is only when you look back that you can see that what you had thought was a "wrong turn" has brought you to exactly the right place and that every step was a right one after all!

Here Is
Some Wisdom for
Your Journey

as You Follow
Life's Path

No matter where life takes you or what path you choose, you will always meet challenges... that is the way life is. There are no guarantees, and no matter how many things you do right or how many rules you follow, there will always be that fork in the road that makes you choose between this way or that. Whenever you meet this place, remember these things: You are loved... love will sustain you. You are strong... prayer will get you through anything. You are wise... the greatest gift of all lies within you.

As a parent, I tried to teach you so many important things about life... to be on time, to be committed, to work hard, to give your best, to love completely, to sacrifice, and, no matter what, to trust in God. I tried to demonstrate the difference between being successful and just getting through.

I tried to show you that love is found in commitment and that sacrifice does make you stronger. I tried to teach you the beautiful reward that is found in giving and also that everything happens for a reason, even if we never understand it. And I tried to give you unending love, which to me is the most important lesson of all!

FAITH
♥
HOPE
♥
LOVE
♥

If You Ever
Get Discouraged...

Hang In There

Remember I am thinking of you...
believing in you... praying for you...
and hoping you know that no
matter how big a problem seems
or how hopeless you feel, you are
never alone, as God's grace is only
one request away!

When you need encouragement, remember these things:

You are stronger than you realize.

Life's inevitable adversities call forth our courage.

You have a lot of wisdom inside you.

God's plan will unfold with
perfect timing.

The voice of your soul will lead
the way.

A hug from my heart is only
a phone call away!

Believe in Miracles

Angels Are Everywhere!

Sometimes we feel that we are all alone, as life brings us challenges to overcome and hardships to bear. But when we least expect it, help can appear. It may be a kind word from a stranger or a phone call at just the right time, and we are suddenly surrounded with the loving grace of God. Miracles happen every day because angels are everywhere.

You are always in my prayers,
and I want you to remember that
so you will be open to the grace
that comes your way. I have asked
that you feel the love of God like
a gentle breeze when you need
inspiration... that your faith remain
unwavering through all of life's
challenges... and that hope be the
burning light that always guides
your way.

10 Simple Things to Remember

1. Love is why we are here.

2. The most important day is today.

3. If you always do your best, you will not have regrets.

4. In spite of your best efforts, some things are just out of your control.

5. Things will always look better tomorrow.

6. Sometimes a wrong turn will bring you to exactly the right place.

7. Sometimes when you think the answer is "no," it is just "not yet."

8. True friends share your joy, see the best in you, and support you through your challenges.

9. God and your parents will always love you.

10. For all your accomplishments, nothing will bring you more happiness than the love you find.

Always Follow
Your Heart

H♥me

Home Is Where
Dreams Come True!

Listen for that voice inside guiding you toward the right thing to do, the right path to travel, and the knowledge of what will bring you happiness and fulfillment. That voice is very quiet, like a whisper. Over time, and mostly through the challenges in life, you will learn to hear it more clearly. Whenever you feel that tug to do something new, help someone in need, or share what you have learned, listen carefully... and follow your heart toward your dreams.

cultivate Your
Unique Talents...

and Let Your
Inner Light
Shine

★

Success is an opportunity
to recognize our talents and
strengths, remembering that
these are both a gift and
a responsibility. When you
work hard and accept life's
ups and downs one day at
a time, you will be rewarded
with the experience of "who
you are."

★

★

When Good
Things come into
Your Life,
Remember to...

Love always returns
to renew the spirit.

Pass Them On!

44

We each have a chance to brighten the day of another. It can be a kind smile... a simple hello... shared inspiration... or an unexpected gesture to let someone know that their being in the world makes a difference. When good things come into your life, I hope you'll be inspired to brighten the day of another. Pass them on!

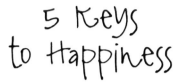

5 Keys
to Happiness

1. Realize that happiness is a choice...
   you can make the decision to "be
   happy" each day.

2. Remember that happiness is contagious.
   Make someone smile, and the good
   feelings come right back to you.

3. Be grateful for the little things in
   life that are free. Make a list, and
   add to it each morning.

4. Believe that ultimately everything happens for a reason. Acceptance leads the way to happiness.

5. Give away some courage every day! When you encourage another to "keep going," "hang in there," or "believe in their dreams," you will find an unending source of happiness.

Hold On to
Friends

Time Spent
With Friends
creates Lifelong
Sweet Memories

Friendship is one of life's greatest treasures, and it is a gift that lasts a lifetime. We create bonds during times in our lives when our beliefs and our experiences are shaping who we are. Those bonds cannot be broken by the passing of time, even when life gets so busy that we lose touch. Let friends know that you think of them often... and they will always have a special place in your heart.

Hold On to Family

Time Spent With Loved Ones creates an Everlasting Bond

Your life holds for you endless possibilities. You have built a solid foundation, and you have worked hard for it. Continue to do what is necessary to move forward one day at a time. Write down your dream and tuck it away — entrusting that all things will come at the right time. Keep sight always of what is important in life.

Remember that true happiness and purpose will be found in relationships — in the workplace and at home. Live each day open to guidance, and your purpose will be revealed to you...

Remember that you are special. There are talents locked away inside you just waiting for the right time to unfold.

Remember that dreams are the start of every great adventure. When you close your eyes and imagine your happy and successful self in the future, you are beginning your journey!

Remember to listen to your heart...
it is where your courage lies. When
you follow your heart, you may meet
challenges, but each of your steps
will be guided.

Remember that "today" is always
the most important day. Enjoy every
moment of it, and may your dreams
come true!

Hold On to Love

It's Why
We Are All
Here After All!

Hold hands with the one you love, no matter how old you are. Say "I love you" every day. Write love notes for your special someone to find. Forget mistakes. Forgive words spoken too soon. Plan time alone together. Focus on the things you like about each other. Do not expect perfection. Try to be the person of your dreams. Support each other through life's challenges. Say "thank you"... everyone needs to be appreciated. Send e-mails that say "I love you." Take walks together. Hug and kiss every day.

Love Is the Gift
I Receive Every Day

Because You Are My
Daughter

You have given me so much to be thankful for as I watch you move through life and develop all the qualities that make you so beautiful. Your shining spirit fills my heart and makes me so proud to call you my daughter. I love you.

I've Always Wanted
All These Things for You...

The knowledge of all the goodness you hold inside... a glimpse of the beautiful spirit that others see... that you find your way in this sometimes confusing world... that you have the good fortune to know the gifts that are yours to share...

That you be given the opportunity
to connect with others in a way
that makes life worth living... that
you have the strength to face any
challenge that comes your way, the
conviction to stand up for what you
believe, and the fortitude to persevere
in the most difficult of circumstances...
and that you always remember you are
loved each and every day.

May You Be Blessed with

Faith, Hope, and Love

May you be blessed with all the good things in life... faith, hope, love, and the blessing of good friends. If you have these things, whatever challenges life brings, you will get through. Your faith will light your path... hope will keep you strong... the love you give to others will bring you joy... and your friendships will remind you of what is important in life.

I couldn't Be More Proud

of you

When you were just a song in my heart, I wanted you... When you were just a babe in my womb, I loved you... When you were only one day old, I knew my life had changed forever. Thank you for your love that brightens my life and for the "gift of you" that makes me so proud. The love and joy and pride I feel because you are my daughter give me rewards that cannot be measured.

Daughter, These Are

My Promises to You

I promise...

To always love you...

To always care about your happiness...

To support your dreams and encourage all the talents that you have inside...

To remember that your dreams were written in the stars and pressed upon your heart long ago...

I promise...

To encourage you to always try...

To remind you to do your best
because that is the most you can do...

To be there when you need me...

To support you when you make mistakes...

To listen when you need to talk...

To be your friend when you need one...

To be your parent forever...

To remind you that the best things in life are free...

To take the "journey of life" with you... sharing birthdays and holidays, triumphs and sadness, the good and the bad, today and tomorrow, and all of the things that bind us together forever.

In the Deepest Part of My Heart

There Is a Special Place Just for You

With all my heart I love you, and I wish you the very best that life can bring.

With all my soul I pray for you, and I ask that your guardian angel always keep you safe and inspired.

With all my being I hope that you always know you are loved... that you always remember you are a child of God... and that in the deepest part of your being, you know my love will always be with you.

I Am So
Grateful to You

for Sharing Your
Beautiful Spirit
With Me

When I became a parent, I expected to become a teacher, as I believed it was my job to guide you through life. I have found, though, that I have been given a wonderful gift, as I have had the opportunity to learn about unconditional love. I have learned to "let go" and trust you to find your way. Thank you for that opportunity and for sharing your beautiful spirit with me.

Wasn't it just yesterday that you were a baby in my arms? I looked at your precious face and wondered where life would take you. Today, I look at the person you've become... strong, kind, thoughtful, caring, and optimistic, and I realize that the dreams I held in my heart for you are alive in your beautiful spirit.

Some days we just need a hand to hold... Some days we just need a hug... Some days we just need a word of encouragement... Some days we just need someone to be there for a laugh and a memory... On my "some days" there is you! Thank you for all the good things you bring to my life!

Give Yourself
a Hug Today

from Me!

"I love you," and I want you to always remember what you mean to me. The joys we have shared and the memories we have made through our lives are a gift beyond measure. Thank you for your love. Today, consider yourself hugged!

Thank You
for Making a

Beautiful Difference
in My Life

For the many kind words you
have spoken, for the thoughtful
things you have done, for the
way you are always there sharing
the special person you are...
your kind and generous spirit
shines brightly in my life, and
I thank you.

There have never been words
more powerful than
"I love you"...
or more meaningful than
"Thank you"...
or more sustaining than
"I believe in you"...
So I'm saying these things to you now:
"I love you more than words can say.
I am so thankful you are a part of my life.
And no matter what,
I will always believe in you!"

Daughter...

You Are
Amazing

When I look at you and how you've grown, I feel so proud. It's not just the beauty in your face but your shining spirit that lights up my world! I don't know where the time has gone... or when yesterday became today... but each time I think of the joy you are in my life, all that comes to mind is "You are amazing!"

These Are the Things I Wish for You

I wish you a life filled with love... a true love to share your every dream... family love to warm your heart... and priceless love found in the gift of friendship.

I wish you peace... peace in knowing who you are... peace in knowing what you believe in... and peace in the understanding of what is important in life.

I wish you joy... joy as you awaken each day with gratitude in your heart for new beginnings... joy when you surrender to the beauty of a flower or a baby's smile... and joy, a hundred times returned, for each time you've brought happiness to another's heart.

Wherever You Go in Life, Daughter...

Please Carry These Words With You

I am so proud of the beautiful spirit I see in you. Loving you has enriched my life in ways that are hard to describe... Your love will always be in my heart and mine in yours. The bond we have found is as everlasting as the spirit.

You are always in my heart and never far from my thoughts, because on the day you were born, I promised to love you forever. My wish is that you find a place in the world that gives you a sense of contribution... that you find the kind of love that makes the stars shine brighter... and that you know the gift of gratitude that comes with living a life of compassion. Remember, wherever you are, whatever you do, wherever life takes you, I will always love you.

About Marci

Marci began her career by hand painting floral designs on clothing. No one was more surprised than she was when one day, in a single burst of inspiration and a completely new and different art style, her delightful characters sprang from her pen! "Their wild and crazy hair is a sign of strength," she thought, "and their crooked little smiles are endearing." She quickly identified the charming characters as Mother, Daughter, Sister, Father, Son, Friend, and so on until all the people and places in life were filled. Then, with her own loved ones in mind, she wrote a true and special sentiment to each one. This would be the beginning of a wonderful success story, which today still finds Marci writing each and every one of her verses in this same personal way.

Marci is a self-taught artist who has always enjoyed writing and art. She is thrilled to see how her delightful characters and universal messages of love have touched the hearts and lives of people everywhere. Her distinctive designs can also be found on Blue Mountain Arts greeting cards, calendars, bookmarks, and other gift items.

To learn more about Marci, look for Children of the Inner Light on Facebook or visit her website: WWW.MARCIonline.com.